QUOTABLE
BILLY GRAHAM

QUOTABLE BILLY GRAHAM

*Words of faith, devotion, and salvation
by and about the Ministry of Billy Graham,
an Evangelist for the World*

JENNIFER BRIGGS KASKI

TESTAMENT BOOKS • NEW YORK

This 2005 edition is published by Testament Books, an imprint of Random
House Value Publishing, a division of Random House, Inc., New York, by
arrangement with TowleHouse Publishing.

Random House
New York • Toronto • London • Sydney • Auckland
www.randomhouse.com

Page design by Mike Towle

Printed in the U.S.A.

Library of Congress Cataloging-in-Publication Data

Graham, Billy, 1918-
    Quotable Billy Graham : words of faith, devotion, and salvation : by and
    about the ministry of Billy Graham, an evangelist for the world / [compiled
    by] Jennifer Briggs Kaski.
        p. cm.
    Originally published: Nashville, Tenn. : TowleHouse Pub., c2002, in series:
    Potent quotables.
    Includes bibliographical references.
    ISBN 0-517-22591-3
    1. Graham, Billy, 1918—Quotations. 2. Christianity—Quotations,
maxims, etc. 3. Graham, Billy, 1918- I. Kaski, Jennifer Briggs. II. Title.

BV3785.G69A3 2004
30'.6—dc22
                                                        2004063789

10 9 8 7 6 5 4 3 2

Contents

Preface

A special thank-you to Dr. Timm England and the staff of the Cedar Hill Veterinary Clinic, who helped my husband Joe and me tremendously in enduring the slow cancer death of our six-year-old dog, Hershizer.

Watching Hersh slowly die before my eyes was very taxing on the process of creating and writing this book, a book important to me because of the magnitude of the man represented in these pages.

Hersh stayed with me, at my feet, as I worked toward many deadlines through the years. She had an amazing life. She river rafted, chased squirrels, stayed with me while I redecorated the church bathroom late at night, and once sat in the front pew at mass. And who else but Hersh, wearing her little Polar Paws, would sit with me while ice fishing?

She went to all my book signings, once wandering into the café when the oatmeal cookies came out of the oven.

The day she died, I knew it was going to happen. Her once bouncing, mid-sized frame had been reduced to bones and fur. I pulled her into my arms and carried her upstairs to my office, where she died at my feet a few hours later as I wrote this book.

Thank you Hersh, wherever you are, for always being here.

Introduction

$\mathcal{H}$e always thought he would die young. So he lived hard, but not by sex, drugs, and alcohol. Since his teenage years, he has done it by preaching about Jesus Christ. He has proselytized to prostitutes and drunks in the bar districts of the small towns of his youth. In adulthood, he has preached to presidents, prime ministers, and plumbers, hopping from country to country.

In youth, when there was no audience, he'd find an old shed outside town and make altar calls to the spiders. Or maybe he would paddle a canoe into the middle of the lake, and preach to the perch.

Graham's a simple, humble man, born on a farm. He's a man committed to God who has wondered out loud, in his somewhat humorous, self-deprecating manner, if God will tell him he's in the wrong place when he gets to heaven.

He has preached to more than a hundred million people, from tents to cathedrals to stadiums. About three million people have answered his urgent admonitions to accept Jesus Christ as their Lord and Savior. A 1995 crusade in Puerto Rico was translated into 116 languages and watched by 1.5 billion people.

All this by a man born in 1918, who has never held office, scored a touchdown, cut a CD, made a movie, or pocketed a million in a year. Yet he has made Gallup's list of the world's ten most-admired men forty-one times in fifty-three years. His book *Angels* sold a million copies in ninety days in 1975. He was presented with America's 114th Congressional Medal of Freedom.

Graham never earned a doctorate, and he has pastored only one church, a small Baptist church in Illinois. That was more than fifty years ago. He takes no offerings. He won't accept money for speeches.

Billy Graham is in the world but not of it. The six-foot-two frame is a little more stooped these days, the sky-blue irises a little cloudier. The strong jaw and the circles below the eyes are there just as they have been since adolescence.

His blond mullet has grown gray while he has evangelized his way through eleven presidents, countless crusades, five children, nineteen grandchildren, and eight great-grandchildren (at last count). He can still console a nation, like he did at a memorial service after the tragic events of September 11, 2001. He had to be helped up the steps of the National Cathedral that day, then helped a nation take its first baby steps toward recovery.

He has been called America's Preacher, and that is apt. But the whole world has listened.

These are the words of Billy Graham.

1
Young Man

When I first came to you I didn't use lofty words and brilliant ideas to tell you God's message. For I decided to concentrate only on Jesus Christ and His death on the cross. I came to you in weakness—timid and trembling, and my message and my preaching were very plain. I did not use wise and persuasive speech but the Holy Spirit was powerful among you.

—I Corinthians 2:1-4

H is dad was a farmer. Billy would probably still be milking cows, too, if a calling hadn't been germinating.

The man who would move the world was a so-so student who wanted to play in the big leagues, and had little burning interest in religion, organized or otherwise.

One day in 1934, thirty or so of the local farmers got together on the Graham farm for a day of prayer for their plight in the depression. When he got home from school and he and his friends saw the group, Graham said, "Oh, I guess they're just some fanatics who talked Dad into letting them use the place."

He liked the ladies and by all accounts the ladies liked the tall, blue-eyed country boy.

After his conversion, he was turned down for membership in a church youth group because he was just too worldly.

After graduation from high school, he went to Bob Jones College, a stringent southern institution where even talks with the opposite sex were conducted under supervision from a chaperone.

Graham couldn't take the rules, was almost expelled, and saved them the trouble by leaving.

3

He fled to the Florida Bible Institute where he could hold hands, play golf, and canoe.

He began dating Emily Cavanaugh and wanted desperately to marry her. She broke it off. It hit him so hard, he retreated into an intense self-examination to seek what God intended for him to be.

He practiced sermons in old sheds or canoes in the middle of the lake.

He ate a pound of butter a day to add weight.

He preached anywhere he could find—country churches in need of a preacher, to drunks and prostitutes on the street, anyone who would listen to him practice.

An act of Congress in 1952 allowed him to become the first person to preach on the steps of the Capitol.

Just another beginning to a life that proves, once again, there are seldom few indicators of greatness.

THERE WAS NEVER ANY QUIETNESS ABOUT BILLY. HE WAS
ALWAYS TUMBLING OVER SOMETHING. HE WAS A HANDFUL. I
WAS RELIEVED WHEN HE STARTED SCHOOL.[1]

—*Graham's mother,* **Morrow**

HE NEVER WEARS DOWN. IT'S JUST THE WAY HE'S BUILT.[2]

—*doctor's words to Graham's parents when
they had him examined for his active nature*

$\mathcal{H}$ere comes Daddy, Sugar Baby.[3]

—*Graham's first sentence*

YOU COULDN'T GET MAD AT THE SKINNY SO-AND-SO.[4]

—*a **school bus driver** who put up with Graham, who
would often cut off the bus's external gas valve so it
would break down right after the Graham kids got off*

HE JUST LIKED EVERYBODY SO ENTHUSIASTICALLY THAT
EVERYBODY HAD TO LIKE HIM. IT WAS JUST A LOVEABLE
FEELING THAT HE HIMSELF SEEMED TO HAVE FOR EVERYBODY.
YOU COULDN'T RESIST HIM.[5]

—*a **classmate***

YOU REALLY TAKING HIM? I'LL GIVE HIM TWO WEEKS TO
WIRE HOME FOR MONEY.[6]

—*Graham's **Uncle Clyde**, who knew Graham's distaste for hard work, as
Graham left to work for a family friend as a Fuller Brush salesman in 1936*

Sincerity is the biggest part of selling anything, including the Christian plan of salvation. Selling those (Fuller) brushes became a cause to me. I was dedicated to it, and the money became secondary. I felt that every family ought to have Fuller Brushes as a matter of principle.[7]

BILLY'S CLASSWORK WAS A SHAMBLES.[8]

—**college friend**, *on the college-age Graham*

BILLY ALWAYS WANTED TO DO SOMETHING BIG. HE DIDN'T KNOW EXACTLY WHAT YET, BUT HE COULDN'T WAIT JUST TO DO SOMETHING BIG, WHATEVER IT WAS.[9]

—**one of Graham's college professors**

*H*ear Billy Graham.[10]

—a sign Graham paid a painter $2.10 (more than two-thirds of the love offering he received) to advertise his appearance at a mission church in the forties

*H*ave you heard the young man with a burning message?[11]

—from a self-distributed flier he made to advertise himself in the forties

8

TO BE WITH BILL IN (EVANGELISTIC) WORK WON'T BE EASY. THERE WILL BE LITTLE FINANCIAL BACKING, LOTS OF OBSTACLES AND CRITICISM AND NO EARTHLY GLORY WHATSOEVER.[12]

—*Ruth, in a July 1941 letter to her parents*

Billy Graham, One of America's Most Outstanding Young Evangelists—Dynamic Messages You Will Never Forget.[13]

—*from a self-distributed flier he made to advertise himself in the forties*

THE PRINTER SAID BILLY HAD ORDERED A THOUSAND FLIERS FOR THAT LITTLE TWO-HUNDRED-PERSON COMMUNITY. HE WAS READY TO GO AFTER IT.[14]

—*a **friend**'s recollection of Graham's zeal for an event that never happened*

9

BILLY'S NOT A PASTOR. THIS KIND OF THING IS VERY HARD NOT FOR HIM TO DO—BUT TO LIKE. HE'D RATHER PREACH AND BE IN ASSOCIATION WITH OTHER MEN WHO WERE PREACHING.[15]

> —a **friend**'s observation on Billy's pastoral work
> in his first and only pastorate, in the early forties

IMAGINE, THAT'S OUR BILLY FRANK.[16]

> —**Graham's parents**, in the early forties, as
> they sat by the car radio listening to their son preach

SWASHBUCKLING SOUTHERNER.[17]

> —**writer**'s description of the crusading evangelist

I never wrote him. I never thanked him. I never had any correspondence or telegrams or anything else. I suppose I could have met him, but I never thought he would see a person like me at that time.[18]

—*on the William R. Hearst endorsement
that sent his career to a higher level*

Sixth Great Sin-Smashing Week.

—*another evangelistic campaign sign for Graham from the forties*

NO ONE SINCE BILLY SUNDAY HAS WIELDED THE REVIVAL SICKLE WITH SUCH SUCCESS AS THIS THIRTY-ONE-YEAR-OLD BLOND TRUMPET-LUNGED NORTH CAROLINIAN.[19]

—**Time** *magazine*

11

I'm glad to see so many of you out this afternoon. I was a sinner and a no-good. I didn't care anything about God, the Bible, or people. Jesus changed my life. He gave me peace and joy. He can give you peace and joy. He will forgive your sins as He forgave mine if you will only let Him into your heart. Jesus died so he could take your sins on His shoulders.[20]

—loosely accepted as Graham's first "sermon," as a teen, talking to prisoners, when a preacher asked him to visit a jail with him

HE WAS IN LOVE WITH A DIFFERENT GIRL EVERY DAY. HE REALLY DID LIKE THE GIRLS. AND THEY LIKED HIM.[21]

*—**Catherine Graham**, his sister*

I never went any further (than enjoying the company of girls). I never touched another woman 'til I was married, in any way beyond kissing.[22]

I HAD NEVER HEARD ANYONE PRAY LIKE THAT BEFORE. I SENSED THAT HERE WAS A MAN THAT KNEW GOD IN A VERY UNUSUAL WAY.[23]

—*Ruth*, on her first impressions of young Billy

WE WERE JUST THESE DYNAMIC, HANDSOME GUYS, YOU KNOW, FULL OF INCREDIBLE ENERGY, FULL OF VITALITY, AND WE WERE TOTALLY COMMITTED . . . EVERY ONE OF US. WE REALLY THOUGHT WE WERE INVOLVED IN A DRAMATIC NEW RESURGENCE OF REVIVALISM OVER THE COUNTRY.[24]

—*Graham colleague*, on the early years of the crusade

THIS IS WHAT I HOPED WOULD HAPPEN IN AMERICA.[25]

—*Harry Truman*, on Graham's youth movement

A YOUNG ATHLETE WITH A TWENTIETH-CENTURY GOSPEL
MESSAGE . . . TERRIFIC PROGRAMS PACED TO A TEENAGE
TEMPO . . . FASTMOVING . . . ENJOYABLE . . . CAPTIVATING.[26]
—*Youth for Christ brochure* touting the evangelist

*A*merican youth must have a hero. It may be a football player, a general in the army, or some other glam-
orous person. Jesus Christ is the hero of my soul and
the coach of my life.[27]

PREACHER.[28]
—*college classmates'* nickname for Graham

14

'The Gospel in my hands became a hammer and a flame. I felt as though I had a rapier in my hands, and through the power of the Bible was slashing deeply into men's consciousness, leading them to surrender to God.[29]

—*reflecting on his early ministry*

*I*n Tampa, Florida, if you go there you'll see a sign that's been put there by Bob Graham (then) governor of Florida . . . this historical marker . . . where I used to speak as many as seven times on a Sunday on the street corner and in the saloons.[30]

15

*W*e are going to sit around the fireplace and have parties, and the angels will wait on us, and we'll drive down the golden streets in a yellow Cadillac convertible.[31]

—a sermon from his early, somewhat less spiritually mature days

I think heaven is going to be a place beyond anything we can imagine, or anyone in Hollywood or on Broadway can imagine. There is a passage in Revelation that says we will serve God in heaven. We're not going to have somebody fan us or sit around on a beach somewhere.[32]

—revised view of heaven, a few years down the road

AT BEST YOU COULD BE A POOR COUNTRY BAPTIST PREACHER
SOMEWHERE OUT IN THE STICKS.[33]
> —**Bob Jones** *of Bob Jones College, when Graham dropped out of school*

They have a place there where the saloon-keeper threw me out into a ditch (laughing) and told me never to come back. And he was there—he's an old man now—but he remembered when he did that. I mean he was there at the dedication of this historical monument. Those were great experiences that taught me a great deal, and I'm very grateful for people who put up with me in those days, and listened to my sermons.[34]

A young Billy Graham, about the time he embarked on his journey to tell people about Jesus Christ. (Photo courtesy of Billy Graham Evangelistic Association)

2
Man of Faith

People are declared righteous because of their faith, not because of their work.
—Romans 4:45

W here does anyone begin to speak about the word faith *in a man like Billy Graham, when this word has been the focal point and the tug against the human will that has defined this man's entire adult life?*

Faith is more than an intellectual belief in a God, or the Holy Trinity, or even the resurrection. Faith is a belief in things not seen—a true belief in the heart vs. a belief in what appears historically accurate.

Many people outside the Christian faith assume that a person of faith is someone who has it all together, spiritually and emotionally. They assume that a person of faith is easily able to handle the ups and downs of life. Especially a person like Billy Graham.

Graham has struggled with faith most of his life, as he has said over and over again. The man of faith who has been a model of this intangible commodity to millions, often questions how good he is, how right or moral he is, or just how much a man of faith he is.

But to the millions who have received faith by the power of his words, his faith is uncompromising.

I heard about a little boy that was flying a kite many years ago, and some people were standing around watching him. They said to him, "What are you doing?" He said, "I am flying a kite."

It flew so high it went into the atmosphere and people said, "We don't see it."

And they asked, "Well, how do you know it's up there?"

He said, "I can feel the tug on the string."

And that's the way we go about knowing God in our lives. We may not see Him, but we can feel the tug in our hearts.[1]

*H*e's the greatest person in the history of mankind and the universe. We can't prove it. I can't put it in a test tube or an astronomical formula, but by faith I believe it because the Bible teaches it.[2]

—*on Jesus*

I remember I went out into the woods . . . about five thousand to six thousand feet up in the Sierras [it was] very beautiful . . . and I went up one moonlit night and opened my Bible. I said, "Lord, I don't understand all that's in this book. But I accept it by faith as your word," and I've never departed from that. I accept it by faith.[3]

—*on a time in his twenties, when he questioned the reality of God*

'The Bible is a message to you. And if you live according to that, He has a plan for you, and the ultimate end of that plan is total happiness, and joy, and peace, and the solution to your problems.[4]

It makes no difference if you are the king of Babylon or the president, or anybody important. He (God) don't care how big your name is or whether you came over on the *Mayflower.*[5]

'The world was ready for Christ . . . because the human race had tried all kinds of religions and philosophies by then—and yet none of them had been able to satisfy the deepest longings of the human heart or take away the burden of guilt. While many still rejected Him, others were open to Christ's message of hope and new life.[6]

—on why Jesus entered the world when he did

If a man blatantly denies the deity of Christ or that Christ has come to the flesh, we are not to even bid him Godspeed. Thus the Scriptures teach that we are to be separated from those who deny the deity of our Lord Jesus Christ. . . . I am to treat him as an Antichrist and an enemy of the cross.[7]

It's something God has given me and us. That's called faith, that we can believe that which we can't understand. I don't understand why God never had a beginning. I don't understand why God has no end, according to the Bible. I don't understand the galaxies that we're discovering through Hubble or the comet. I stood and watched it the other night in absolute amazement, and thinking of all the things I'd read about it. I don't understand that, but I accept it by faith that it's true.[8]

*S*imply going to church doesn't make you a Christian; you become a Christian only by making a personal commitment of your life to Jesus Christ and by faith asking Him to come into your heart.[9]

I believe the way of salvation is through Christ. He said, "I am the way, the truth, and the life, and no man comes to the Father but by Me." I think that's in the hands of God. I can't make that judgment.[10]

—*on the fate of Jews, Muslims, Buddhists, etc.*

*W*e have people who claim to be Christian who don't live it, who don't walk with Christ, and I think that's one of the great stumbling blocks that we have in the church today. That was a great problem in the early church and throughout the history of the church.[11]

I'm not going to heaven because I'm good. I'm not going to heaven because I preach to a lot of people. I'm going to heaven because of God's grace and mercy in Christ on the Cross. I haven't worked for it. It's a free gift from God for me.[12]

*W*ait 'til those gravestones start popping like popcorn in a popper. Oh boy, won't it be wonderful when those gravestones start popping?[13]

—*on Christ's eventual return to earth*

*T*here's so many things I don't understand. I don't understand God. I don't understand the fact that I have a beginning and He has no end. I don't understand how the blood of Jesus Christ can cleanse me from my sins. The Scripture says that, so I take it by faith. You know the doubts can be resolved saying, "I don't understand it, and I can't prove it scientifically, but I believe it."[14]

I would think that was after I received Christ and had answered His call to preach in Florida, and my girl-friend left me and I was very much in love with her— in fact, we were sort of unofficially engaged, and she took up with another fellow and that was a crisis to me. And I went to the Lord in prayer and committed it to the Lord and I didn't get over it until, really, I met Ruth about two years later.[15]

—*on the time in his life he was tested most*

*T*here's a difference between an intellectual faith and a personal, heart faith in which I opened my heart to Him and let Him rule my life.[16]

I believe there's a hell, but I think hell has been misunderstood. I think that hell is separation from God. And, of course, to me, that would be hell.[17]

It's February 1952, and Graham is preaching in front of the U.S. Capitol, reportedly proclaiming, "There is a hunger for God today." (AP/Wide World)

3
Common Man

Where did He get all his wisdom and the power to perform such miracles? He's just the carpenter, the son of Mary and brother of James, Joseph, Judas, and Simon. And His sisters live right here among us.

—Mark 6:23

*I*n a 1997 interview with Midwest Today, *Graham spoke of going to a football game and getting to sit in the skybox with the owners.*

Here is a man of world concern who gets a charge out of freebie seats in a luxury box.

Billy Graham came from a regular farming family in North Carolina, and he figures he'd still be farming today if life hadn't turned out so incredibly different from the days of 5:00 A.M. cow-milking calls.

His children were a little on the wild side. They straightened out like most kids do, and they went out into the world and got jobs like most grownups do.

The man, who has flown around the world, has been through his share of fast-food drive-throughs.

He disdains the suit just like the next guy, and he wears blue jeans just about every single day.

He likes nice hotels and ornery great-grandkids.

Fame and faith have not dehumanized this regular guy.

33

I think somewhere along the line, somebody exaggerated. I sincerely believe that.[1]

—*on being named one of* Time'*s most-influential people*

*N*ewspapers and television have made me out to be a saint. I'm not. I'm not a Mother Teresa, and I feel that very much.[2]

I lived on a farm (as a kid). The only difference (between then and now) was I had to get up early in the morning and go milk cows. When I came back from school that day, I had to milk those same cows. There were about twenty cows I had to milk. By hand. That was before they had those machines. I loved being a farmer. But God called me to this work that I'm in now. I knew it was God calling. I said, "Yes, I will follow what God wants me to do."[3]

*A*s far as day-to-day friendship and being together at various functions (with nonbelievers), I don't think that there should be any difference at all. I have many friends that don't claim to be followers of Christ.[4]

*H*as God ever said to you, "Billy, you're too full of yourself. You have to remember who's in charge here?" Well, I've said that to myself a billion times in my heart, because I know God is in charge. Not me, I'm nothing. I wouldn't be anything except for the power of the spirit of God.[5]

I wear blue jeans all day long, even when I'm traveling and going to a hotel. In the hotel room I always wear blue jeans. This coat I've had for about twenty-something years, given to me by Johnny Cash.[6]

WHEN BILL FINDS OUT THAT HEAVEN IS NOT LIKE A HOLIDAY INN OR A MARRIOTT, HE'LL BE BACK.[7]

> —*Ruth*, on Billy's frequent absences from home while taking his ministry to the world

*W*hen I get there (heaven), I'm sure that Jesus is going to say He will welcome me. But I think that He's going to say, "Well done, our good and faithful servant." Or He may say, "You're in the wrong place."[8]

> —*an example of his unique brand of self-deprecating humor*

HE BROADCAST WITH A GREAT ENTHUSIASM AND KNOWLEDGE OF THE GAME.[9]

> —*Charlie Finley*, former baseball owner, assessing Graham's impromptu and credible turn doing radio play-by-play for an Oakland A's baseball game

*P*eople put me on a pedestal that I don't belong in my personal life.[10]

4
Preacher Man

I am not teaching my own ideas, but those of God who sent me. Anyone who wants to do the will of God will know whether my teaching is from God or is merely my own.

—John 7:16-17

*I*n 1997 the skies were pouring out cold wet drops on the seventy-five thousand who had come to hear Graham preach. Undaunted, he walked up to the mike, requested quiet, then told the soaked masses that God would make a dry hole above them.

Graham looked toward the sky, and the rain stopped.

From his youth, he began mapping a road to the pulpit. It would be a hard highway of separation from his wife while he connected with the world, saving souls while losing his children's youth.

It would call for preparation and prayer so intense that, even in healthier days, it left him almost limp by the time the altar call came around.

Someday, when Billy Graham has left this earth and gone to the next great adventure, the world will picture him in a pulpit, the memory of the thick, powerful drawl lingering like a found artifact.

His work has called him to be a father, a husband, a businessman, and a negotiator, but in the ultimate worldview, this evangelist is the consummate preacher.

*L*ife is uncertain. God does not give us the date of our death. I'm going to ask you to get up out of your seat and come and stand here in front of the platform, and say by your coming, "Tonight I want Christ in my heart."

—typical closing remarks to one of his sermons

*J*ust as I am, without one plea,
But that Thy blood was shed for me.
And that Thou bidd'st me to come to Thee,
Oh, Lamb of God, I come, I come.

—from "Just As I Am," the defining song of Graham's crusades (lyrics by Charlotte Elliot, music by William B. Bradbury)

*S*eek good and not evil that you may live.

—one of Graham's most quoted verses in his early years, from Amos 5:14

BUT ON THE NIGHT HE DIED, NOVEMBER 6, 1935, A GANGLY
TEENAGER STROLLED SELF-CONSCIOUSLY INTO AN ITINERANT
EVANGELIST'S TABERNACLE IN CHARLOTTE, NORTH CAROLINA.
HE WAS UNAWARE THE MOST FAMOUS PREACHER IN AMERICA
HAD JUST DIED. AND WHEN HE HIT THE SAWDUST TRAIL LATER
THAT EVENING, NEITHER HE NOR ANYONE WHO WATCHED
HIM STRIDE NERVOUSLY DOWN THE AISLE COULD HAVE SUS-
PECTED THAT THE BOY WHO WOULD BECOME THE MOST
FAMOUS PREACHER OF ALL TIME, HAD JUST GIVEN HIS LIFE TO
JESUS CHRIST.[1]

—*Billy Sunday was the most famous evangelist before Graham.
The night Sunday died, was the same night Graham accepted
Christ. Biographer* **William Martin** *confirmed this coincidence with Graham*

I didn't have any tears; I didn't have any emotion. I
didn't hear any thunder, there was no lightning. But
right there, I made my decision for Christ. It was as
simple as that, and conclusive.[2]

DON'T LET ANYONE THINK LESS OF YOU BECAUSE YOU ARE YOUNG. BE AN EXAMPLE IN WHAT YOU TEACH, IN THE WAY YOU LIVE, IN YOUR LOVE, YOUR FAITH, AND YOUR PURITY.

—I Timothy 4:12

LAST WEEK, IN THE LAKESHORE RESORT OF LAUSANNE, SWITZERLAND, THAT BELIEF (THAT THE CHRISTIAN'S FOREMOST COMMISSION IS TO PREACH THE GOSPEL) FOUND A FORMIDABLE FORUM, POSSIBLY THE WIDEST-RANGING MEETING OF CHRISTIANS EVER HELD. BROUGHT TOGETHER LARGELY THROUGH THE EFFORTS OF REV. BILLY GRAHAM, SOME TWENTY-FOUR HUNDRED PROTESTANT EVANGELICAL LEADERS FROM 150 COUNTRIES ENDED A TEN-DAY INTERNA-TIONAL CONGRESS ON WORLD EVANGELISM THAT SERVED NOTICE OF THE VIGOR OF CONSERVATIVE, RESOLUTELY BIBLICAL, FERVENTLY MISSION-MINDED CHRISTIANITY. (THIS MEETING) CONSTITUTED A CONSIDERABLE CHALLENGE TO THE PREVAILING PHILOSOPHY OF THE WORLD COUNCIL OF CHURCHES, HEADQUARTERED SOME THIRTY MILES DOWN LAKE LEMAN IN GENEVA.[3]

—Time *magazine*

Say I'm preaching to an audience of three or four thousand. I can look straight at them, and I can tell them when a man way back in the auditorium blinks his eyes. When he does that, I know it's time for a change of pace, or I'll lose some of the people. That's what I've trained my voice for.[4]

There have been times. . . . that I've come down from the platform absolutely exhausted. I feel like I've been wrestling with the devil. (At the hymn of invitation) some sort of physical energy goes out of me and I feel terribly weak. I'm depleted.[5]

43

BEING IN THAT STADIUM, SURROUNDED BY ALL THAT EMOTION AND GOOD FEELING, ALL THESE PEOPLE FILLED WITH LOVE. I CAN'T REMEMBER ANY ONE THING HE SAID, JUST THE PRESENCE OF EVERYONE BROUGHT TO WORSHIP WITH THEM. DANA LOOKED AT ME AND SAID, "I'D LIKE TO GO DOWN THERE." WE GRABBED AHOLD OF EACH OTHER'S HAND, AND WE WENT. WE RECOMMITTED OUR LIVES TO CHRIST.[6]

—**Brock Fisher**, *one of millions who have answered a Graham altar call*

I have never had the gift of healing people. Some clergy have said that they have that gift. I have never had it.[7]

God loves you. He has a plan for your life. Nothing happens by accident. Everything is planned by God for a purpose. And that purpose is always good. You see, God is a God of love and mercy. And whatever happens to us is in God's plan.[8]

*W*hat does "God forgives" mean? A priest replied, "It means all your files are deleted." You too can have all your files deleted by the cross. Three days after his agonizing death, something glorious happened. Jesus rose from the dead. That's what God has done for you because He loves you.[9]

I've stuck to the same message. I have different texts, different illustrations and different stories and all the rest, but the Gospel is the Gospel. There's only one Gospel, and the human heart is the same.[10]

I'm sure in the minds of people who are nonreligious, they tend to lump all people who call themselves evangelists together.[11]

—*on the scandals that have plagued other evangelists*

It seems we've gotten caught up in numbers. We have so many polls that give different figures about how many people go to church and synagogue, how many are saved and unsaved. When I ask people to come forward and a thousand people respond, I know in my heart they're not all converted.[12]

*W*orld travel and getting to know clergy of all denominations has helped mold me into an ecumenical being. We're separated by theology, and, in some instances, culture and race, but all of that means nothing to me anymore.[13]

*E*very night when I get up to speak, I just ask the Lord to help me say the right thing, and not to say anything that might lead them astray.[14]

*I*t takes a tremendous amount of energy (to prepare for a crusade). My part is now just preaching. We have a staff of people who do everything, and they're wonderful people and they're dedicated to the Lord. I'm very proud of every one of them.[15]

WE HAVE PEOPLE IN OUR CHURCH TODAY WHO FOUND CHRIST AT BILLY GRAHAM'S LAST LOUISVILLE CRUSADE IN 1956, AND THEY WERE NEVER THE SAME.[16]

—Kevin Ezell, pastor, Highview Baptist Church, Louisville, Kentucky

I think there's a greater emphasis on social issues. A greater emphasis on the love of God.[17]

—*on how his ministry has changed over time*

I stick to the Bible and just preach the Gospel that I think all Christians believe. We center on the cross, the resurrection, and the need to repent of our sins.[18]

I don't think an evangelist can be trained. I think he has to be called by God and raised up by God. I think if the Lord wants other evangelists, He'll raise them up.[19]

5
Globetrotting Man

I urge you, first of all, to pray for all people. As you make your requests, plead for God's mercy and give thanks. Pray this way for kings and all others who are in authority, so that we can live in peace and quietness, in godliness and dignity.

—I Timothy 2:2

*W*hen people picture Billy Graham, they most likely
visualize the chin up, the strong jaw cocked slightly,
clenched fist rising above podium, preaching.

A secondary view might be the man in a casual sweater
and golf shoes, putting with Richard Nixon, or walking a
beach with George W. Bush, or counseling the elder Bush the
night before the Gulf War.

World leaders have hung on his words at banquets.
Tribesmen have welcomed his words.

He has had dealings with every U.S. president since
Truman.

He has preached to the people of Appalachia and the people
of the Soviet Union. He has been called upon by leaders in
times of tragedy.

And it all seems so implausible, out of the generations
who have preached the word of God, from grand coliseums,
and cramped and sweaty tents, from the shores of the Pacific
to the waves of the Atlantic, that this man among all the
others is the one with an unknown something that propelled
him to a position of prominence on par with any public figure
one could name.

Take twelve days in June 1992. He went to Texas to see a dying John Connally. Then it was off to France to hide out for work on his memoirs. Connally died and it was straight back to Texas to preach the funeral. Back to France. Then back to the United States, to California, for Pat Nixon's funeral. Back to France.

He lobbied to Truman to address communism in Korea and encouraged Eisenhower to send in troops to Little Rock to enforce school desegregation.

He has preached the world over, and the world is still listening.

'Believe your great campaign has won moral victory. Am certain God will use you greatly in the future.

—widely publicized telegram to Richard Nixon after Nixon's 1960 presidential-election loss to John F. Kennedy

I was scared to death, but I stood up and tried to walk down the middle line as much as I could.[1]

—on the time Kennedy, without notice at a press conference, asked Graham to answer questions on religious issues

THE REVEREND DR. BILLY GRAHAM DECLARED TONIGHT THAT THE ELECTION OF JOHN F. KENNEDY, A ROMAN CATHOLIC, HAD PROMOTED BETTER UNDERSTANDING BETWEEN THE PROTESTANT AND CATHOLIC CHURCHES IN THE UNITED STATES. DR. GRAHAM, THE EVANGELIST, SAID MR. KENNEDY'S VICTORY PROVED THERE WAS NOT AS MUCH RELIGIOUS PREJUDICE AS MANY HAD FEARED AND PROBABLY HAD REDUCED FOREVER THE IMPORTANCE OF THE RELIGIOUS ISSUE IN AMERICAN ELECTIONS.[2]

—**New York Times**, *following Kennedy's impromptu Graham press conference*

GREATEST PERSON IN THE WORLD TODAY.
—*1976 Miss USA pageant contestants' vote*

1. GOD. 2. BILLY GRAHAM.[3]
—*results of a 1978 Ladies Home Journal poll on "achievements in religion"*

Not only unethical, but criminal. I can make no excuses for Watergate. I condemn it, and I deplore it, and it has hurt America.[4]
—*on his good friend Richard Nixon's downfall*

There's a little bit of Watergate in all of us. Let's don't go around self-righteous talking about all those bad people. Satan was somehow involved in the downfall of Nixon.[5]

GRAHAM MADE A CONSCIOUS EFFORT TO BEFRIEND PEOPLE
IN POWER SO HE COULD GAIN ACCESS TO BIGGER CROWDS.[6]
—**Stephen Winzenburg**, *a professor at Grand View College in
Des Moines, Iowa, who has studied various preachers, including Graham*

We believe that Jesus Christ is coming back to this
earth again someday, and He is going to rule and reign,
and it's going to be an era of glorious and wonderful
peace. It'll be a God-imposed peace. It won't be peace
that we're going to work out on a table in Geneva.[7]

Everybody knows that there is a God or supernatural
power. I sat beside Mrs. Gorbachev once at a dinner at
the White House. Her husband was then in power in
Russia. And I knew that she was an atheist. And I
asked the Russian ambassador what I should talk
about. He said, "Talk to her about religion because
that's what she's really interested in." And I find
everywhere people are interested in religion. They are
interested in talking about God and the supernatural.[8]

57

I HAVE OFTEN TOLD FRIENDS THAT WHEN YOU WENT INTO THE MINISTRY, POLITICS LOST ONE OF ITS POTENTIALLY GREATEST PRACTITIONERS.[9]

—**Nixon**, *in letter to Graham*

They (John F. Kennedy Jr. and his wife) were one of the nicest young couples I have ever met. But when they got on that plane a few months ago, they never dreamed that that would be their last day. Do you know where you are going to spend eternity?[10]

We can't bind up the wounds, but God can, and that's why faith is so important. And Jesus said, "I will be with you always, even to the end of the world."[11]

—*on the trials of the Kennedy family*

'That's something that I, too, can't foresee, but I'm almost certain that it's true.[12]

—on whether John F. Kennedy Jr. went to heaven

HE WOULD NOT WANT TO HEAR IT, HE'S SUCH A HUMBLE MAN, BUT AROUND THE WORLD WE NEED TO SAY IT, "THANK YOU, BILLY GRAHAM."[13]

*—**Pat Boone**, in song*

I'm glad to know that we do have political leaders that believe in God and that has been true from the days of George Washington. I just did a little book on George Washington that they're giving away now to all the visitors at Mount Vernon. And I was myself amazed, in studying once again the life of George Washington, how often he referred to his faith in God.[14]

Workers tackle a mailroom full of promotional material going out for one of the Billy Graham Crusades, this one at Madison Square Garden in New York in the 1950s. (AP/Wide World)

I don't think the Bible is against war if it's a legitimate war. And I remember—I tell the story . . . about being with President Bush the night before the Gulf War began. We talked about that, and he didn't want to go to war. And I haven't talked to any president yet who wanted to go to war.[15]

WITHOUT WISE LEADERSHIP, A NATION FALLS. WITH MANY
COUNSELORS, THERE IS SAFETY.

—Proverbs 11:11

(Ronald) Reagan, I met through his mother-in-law.
She came out to a golf course in Arizona where I was
playing with (publisher) Henry Luce. She asked if I
would meet her new son-in-law, Ronald Reagan. I
said, "You mean the actor?" We've been good friends
ever since.[16]

2YK.[17]

—his reference to Y2K, spoken when
expressing his lack of worry about its arrival

You can preach on any street corner and hand out all the Bibles you can get. They (the people of the former Soviet Union) haven't had Bibles for seventy years, and they are starved for the Gospel, because they know their roots lie deep in Christianity.[18]

I think most presidents are amazed at the overwhelming responsibility they have when they enter office and the tremendous amount of work there is. See, a modern president today has far more responsibility than a president a few years ago. And I personally, if I were rewriting the Constitution or had any part in it, I would suggest . . . that he (the president) would be more like a monarch and then have a prime minister under him.[19]

HE HAS PREACHED TO MORE PEOPLE IN LIVE AUDIENCES THAN ANYONE ELSE IN HISTORY. HIS MINISTRY IS TRULY INTERNATIONAL. DR. GRAHAM HAS BLAZED A TRAIL OF CHRISTIAN COMMITMENT MARKED BY TOLERANCE AND RESPECT FOR OTHERS.[20]

—*Sir Christopher Meyer*, British ambassador, on Graham's knighting in December 2001

I don't eat with beautiful women alone.[21]

—explaining his rationale for having lunch with Hillary Rodham Clinton in a hotel dining room during a 1993 crusade in Little Rock, Arkansas

I HARDLY GO ANYWHERE AS PRESIDENT THAT BILLY GRAHAM HASN'T BEEN THERE FIRST, PREACHING.[22]

—*President Bill Clinton*, after the Grahams were awarded the Congressional Medal of Freedom, May 2, 1996

I said the Mideast would blow up if I went over there. Golda (Meir) then reached under the table and squeezed my hand. She was greatly relieved.[23]

—recalling when Nixon offered him the ambassadorship to Israel at a meeting with Golda Meir

*H*e (Pope John Paul II) has brought the greatest impact of any pope in the last two hundred years. I admire his courage, determination, intellectual abilities, and his understanding of Catholic, Protestant, and Orthodox differences, and the attempt at some form of reconciliation.[24]

*T*he first time I dined with him (Pope John Paul II), we were sitting across the table, and he reached out and touched my hand and said, "We are brothers."[25]

65

*W*hen we had our last crusade in Russia—the only long crusade we've ever held in the Olympic stadium—the place would be jammed hours before the start of the meeting. I would preach the gospel and give an invitation and the first night about half the audience came forward. I said, "Go back to your seats." I thought they'd misunderstood. And then I gave it as straight as I knew how and they still came. It was that way night after night.[26]

I've had the privilege of knowing nine or ten (presidents) and I've known several of them very well, including the present president. Each has influenced me to a certain extent. I suppose I was closer to a few than I was to others. And the first president I knew was (Dwight) Eisenhower, and before he became president he asked me to come to Paris where he was the head of SHAPE (Supreme Headquarters Allied Powers Europe).[27]

*W*hen he (Eisenhower) was nominated he asked me to come to his hotel in Chicago because he thought I could help him write speeches. I think he was soon disillusioned.[28]

*H*e (Eisenhower) did accept some suggestions on religious matters because he did want a spiritual message in his speeches to the American people. Eisenhower was a very religious man.[29]

I remember when President (Lyndon) Johnson thought that I should run for president and he said his organization would back me, or the other party, the same thing. Those were not even temptations. I just said, "I will never do anything in my entire life except preach the Gospel."[30]

'There is a mystery to all this. And I have to frankly tell you that I don't know. And I know that if you have faith in God and put your trust and confidence in Him, this gives you a peace and it settles your life and it gives you joy. And a certainty.[31]

—*on tragedy*

6
Civil Man

There is no longer Jew or Gentile, slave or free, male or female. For you are all Christians—you are one in Christ Jesus.

—Galatians 3:20

*G*raham has made fast acquaintances of presidents and
world leaders, yet he has often strayed from political
hot-button issues, having felt firsthand the backlash such
comments can create.

But, occasionally, he has delved into the realm of the socio-
political, particularly when it comes to views on race.

At a time when it was wildly unpopular, this man of
the South refused to preach to segregated crowds. He removed
the velvet-roped barricades himself in some meeting places of
the 1960s.

Nelson Mandela at one time asked Graham to visit South
Africa because of the impact he felt Graham would have there,
as there were still bad feelings among the races despite the end
of apartheid.

He did not go. That would have been pretty political.

But Graham has no lack of opinion when it comes to the
equality of the races, stewardship of the earth, help for the poor,
his respect for all denominations and faiths, and even life on
other planets.

*I*n 1951, when there was segregating of the audience in Chattanooga, Tennessee, they put ropes up to divide the audience, with the black people sitting behind and the whites sitting up front. I went down and personally removed the ropes.[1]

*H*e and I took two weeks together in Puerto Rico once. Oh, we had a great time. You know, he was a divinity student, he was a clergyman. . . . I think his "Dream" speech in Washington was one of the most eloquent speeches that anybody will ever hear.[2]

—*on his relationship with Dr. Martin Luther King*

*W*hen people asked me what I was going to speak about, I said, "I'm going to preach on the love of God and how we are to love each other." That is the key to solving the race problem in the world.[3]

MY DEAR BROTHERS AND SISTERS. HOW CAN YOU CLAIM
THAT YOU HAVE FAITH IN OUR GLORIOUS LORD JESUS CHRIST
IF YOU FAVOR SOME PEOPLE MORE THAN OTHERS?

—James 2:1

They're God's punk rock children.
—when asked in the eighties about the punk craze

Astrology will never give you the answer to life's deepest
questions—including where you will spend eternity.[4]

Almost every week I get at least one letter from someone whose life has been almost destroyed because of it
(gambling). Don't fool yourself into thinking your luck
will change; the odds are always against you. And don't
think you can stop anytime you want to; you won't.[5]

*Y*ou can walk down the streets of our country in big cities or go to the universities, as I often do, and you sense that they're searching for something, but they don't know what. And I would call this the "searching generation."[6]

—on America's youth

I can identify with them (the religious right) on theology, probably in many areas. But in the political emphasis they have, I don't, because I don't think Jesus or the Apostles took sides in the political arenas of their day.[7]

I think they've (Operation Rescue) gone much too far, and their cause has been hurt. The tactics ought to be prayer and discussion.[8]

Evangelical carries the idea that you believe the Bible, and you believe in the virgin birth of Christ and so forth. There's the other group that could be called radical liberal; they're the group that's way to the left. Then there's the extreme fundamentals. Both of them don't support me, usually, so I feel like I'm on the right track somehow.[9]

When we get there, I don't think we're going to just sit down. I think God will have other work for us to do. There are billions and billions and trillions of other planets and other stars, and I believe there's life on many of those. And I believe God may have a job for us to do on some of those places.[10]

75

Billy Graham sporting sunglasses, with son Franklin standing in back, in Cincinnati in June 2002. (AP/Wide World photo by David Kohl)

Some people just reach the point where they can't make it together, and it would be better for their family and so forth if they were separated. I'm against divorce. I think the Bible teaches that divorce is wrong, but at the same time I also believe that the Bible has a leeway. Jesus said, except for adultery, a person should not be divorced and should not be separated, and I think that is exactly the teaching of the New Testament. But in the Old Testament men could have more than one wife under certain circumstances, and in many religions of the world like Islam you can have three or four wives, and there must be reasons for that, and I think that some of them are valid reasons.[11]

—answering a question about divorce

God said look after his garden, and we are responsible for it.[12]

I used to think that pagans in far-off countries were lost—were going to hell—if they did not have the Gospel of Jesus Christ preached to them. I no longer believe that . . . I believe there are other ways of recognizing the existence of God, through nature, for instance, and plenty of other opportunities, therefore, of saying, "Yes," to God.[13]

7
Man of Prayer

You can be sure of this: The Lord has set apart the Godly for himself. The Lord will answer when I call to Him.

—Psalms 4:3

*W*e picture the man praying all the time. Graham has said he sort of has a constant subconscious dialogue with the Lord. It goes on just about all the time, in the living room of wicker and wood in his mountain home, even in the McDonald's drive-through down the hill.

When the kids were young, to hear the family tell it, Dad did more praying than scolding, though. He and Ruth reflect that she did the scolding and he did more of the praying on those nights when Franklin was out late, or smoking or drinking or getting kicked out of college.

Graham prays before he begins a sermon. The prayer appears so intense that, by the time he finishes his sermon, he says he is emotionally drained beyond the point of exhaustion. Even when he was young and more vigorous, the dialogue with God was so intense, and the force of the spirit that moved him so compelling, that while blessing thousands, he was completely spent though blessed himself, all through the power of prayer.

𝓗e gave us free will because we are made in the image of God. Why He gave it to man, not to other creatures—I don't know the answer to that. There's a mystery to that. We are entering the realm only God can answer.[1]

𝓜any times I've gone to the pulpit and didn't know what I was going to say that evening, didn't know what my first words were going to be. I went there nervous and frightened. . . . I'm always nervous or tense for the first five minutes. I have even prayed, "Now Lord, you take over this service, take over and give me the words to say," and I've sensed the presence and power of God, and I believe that's an answer to prayer.[2]

I do not believe that any prayer is ever forgotten or lost. It may not be answered immediately; it may be answered a generation from now.[3]

⁓

AND WE CAN BE CONFIDENT THAT HE WILL LISTEN TO US WHENEVER WE ASK HIM FOR ANYTHING IN LINE WITH HIS WILL.

—I John 5:14

⁓

I pray for strength to do the work that God has prepared for me that day. Because as I've gotten older, at seventy-eight, you don't have quite the strength you do at thirty-seven or thirty-eight. And so I have to pray, "God, give me the strength for the work You want me to do today."[4]

⁓

8
Man in Love

The man who finds a wife finds a treasure, and receives favor from the Lord.
—Proverbs 18:22

Billy and Ruth Graham on their fiftieth wedding anniversary.
(Photo by Russ Busby)

After meeting Ruth, Billy went home and wrote his mother he had met the woman he would marry because she looked just like her. His mother later burned the letters because she was afraid Ruth would see them someday and be insulted by the comparison.

After a Florida girl he was engaged to dumped him, Billy said he would never kiss another until he knew she would be his wife.

That would be Ruth, the female half of the enduring, unseen love story behind the public face of Billy Graham.

It was a somewhat tumultuous courtship with break-ups and arguments over Ruth's plan to become a missionary, that would culminate in a union People *magazine would someday list in an issue of "Greatest Love Stories."*

Their first date was to Wheaton College's production of Handel's Messiah.

She wore her only dress and some fake pearls. Billy wore a fifteen-dollar suit.

Ruth had some health issues, mainly due to exhaustion. On dates he would change her order from tea to milk, or buy

87

her vitamins instead of flowers. If he found out she hadn't eaten lunch, he'd take her for hot chocolate and a sandwich and literally make her eat every bite.

He thought she had given up the career idea, but Ruth, the daughter of missionaries who grew up in China, had not, and more arguments ensued. It just didn't look like this was ever going to work out, and he didn't want her to know that he loved her so, he'd go with her to the Himalayas if he had to.

Billy kept playing the "Woman was meant to be a wife and mother" card, hoping it would work. This only made Ruth dig her heels in deeper, while keeping her longing for Billy to herself.

Eventually, love won the battle, and it has helped them fight the war for God they wage together.

They were married in Montreat, North Carolina, Presbyterian Church, Friday, August 13, 1943.

The first year, they were so poor they put a red cloth over a light bulb to pretend it was a fireplace.

GOD, IF YOU'LL LET ME SERVE YOU WITH THAT MAN, I'D
CONSIDER IT THE GREATEST PRIVILEGE OF MY LIFE.[1]
            —*Ruth*, *on her knees in the dorm room, after her first date with Billy*

On the greatest event he has witnessed God perform:
When my wife said yes to me when I asked her to
marry me. I had fallen in love with her. But it took
her a year to reciprocate.[2]

She's been a marvelous person to be able to stay here,
raise five children, nineteen grandchildren, and eight
great-grandchildren. She's been the one that's done the
work and kept up with them and talked with them and
loved them, taught them Scriptures and so forth. She
let me travel all over the world preaching the gospel. I
think if there's any secret in our marriage, it's Ruth.
There's very few women I've ever known like her.[3]

OH LOVER, OH BELOVED, EAT AND DRINK! YES, DRINK DEEPLY OF THIS LOVE.

—Song of Songs 5:1

I THINK BEING AN OLD MAID MISSIONARY IS THE HIGHEST CALL THERE IS.[4]

*—**Ruth** to Billy when she realized Billy expected her to give up her career aspirations for him*

*W*oman was created to be a wife and a mother.[5]

—to Ruth, in one of their near deal-ender arguments over her career plans

EVERY TIME THEY GOT BACK TOGETHER, IT WAS LIKE A HONEYMOON. THEY SHARED A LOT OF PHYSICAL LOVE. THAT WAS VERY REASSURING TO ME.[6]

*—daughter **Gigi***

HE WOULD STAND UP EVERY TIME SHE CAME IN THE ROOM.[7]
—**William Martin**, *Graham biographer*

You know, we're still lovers.[8]
—*to biographer William Martin*

THEY DON'T LIKE TO BE SEPARATED BY A LOT OF MILES. THEY JUST LIKE KNOWING THE OTHER ONE'S RIGHT THERE.[9]
—*daughter* **Gigi**

BILLY WAS BROUGHT UP IN A HOUSE WHERE THE WOMAN DID NOT QUESTION THE MEN, WHILE IN THE BELL HOUSE, THAT'S WHAT WE DID.[10]

—**Ruth**

KISS ME AGAIN, FOR YOUR LOVE IS SWEETER THAN WINE.
—*Song of Songs 1:16-17*

I WANTED HIM. I NEEDED HIM. HE WOULD BE COMING TO ME THROUGH THE WOODS AND I WOULD RUN TO MEET HIM AND I WOULD TELL HIM I KNEW, NOW, AND I WOULD YIELD EVERYTHING. AND HE WOULD HOLD ME CLOSE—BUT HE WOULD BE VERY QUIET. AND IT WOULD BE OVER WITH, ALL THIS STRUGGLING AND THINKING AND REASONING, THIS FEVERISH TOSSING TO AND FRO IN MY MIND.[11]

*—**Ruth**, recalling her decision to surrender her career for Billy, while he was out of town*

'Do you think I'm asking you out too much? Because I don't want to embarrass you by taking you out too frequently.[12]

—to Ruth

WHAT A LOVELY, PLEASANT SIGHT YOU ARE, MY LOVE, AS WE LIE HERE ON THE GRASS, SHADED BY CEDAR TREES AND SPREADING FIRS.

—Song of Songs 1:16-17

I haven't tried to win you, Ruth. I haven't asked you to fall in love with me. I haven't sent you candy and flowers and lovely gifts. I have asked the Lord if you are the one, to win you for me. If not, to keep you from falling in love with me.[13]

—comment to Ruth which prompted her to date other men

*E*ither you date just me, or you can date everybody but me.[14]

—comment to Ruth after she started dating other men

I'll lead and you follow.[15]

—trying to talk girlfriend Ruth out of becoming a missionary, so they could marry

(*R*uth) was the one who had the greatest influence in urging me to be an evangelist.

I AM MY LOVER'S, AND MY LOVER IS MINE.

—*Song of Songs 6:3*

*I*t [didn't test] my faith because I knew she was going to be all right whether she lived or died, because she lives halfway in heaven anyway.[16]

—*on Ruth's illness one year*

HOW IN THE WORLD CAN YOU CALL A GROWN MAN, WHO IS SIX-FOOT-TWO, BILLY?[17]

—***Ruth***, *on why she calls him Bill*

94

9
Family Man

Train up a child in the way he should go, and when he is old, he will not depart from it.

—**Proverbs 22:6**

*G*o figure. One son was a long-haired biker, another struggled with an addiction. One daughter aspired to be a model.
How could we take Graham's advice if we didn't know that he, too, waited up until 3:00 A.M. for his prodigals to come home?

Ruth did most of the waiting. While the kids were hitting the teens, Graham was achieving worldwide popularity.

Virginia Leftwich (Gigi), Anne Morrow (Anne), Ruth Bell (Bunny), William Franklin III (Franklin), and Nelson Edman (Ned), had to answer to the woman everyone agrees was the more stern disciplinarian of the two parents.

Of all the kids, Franklin was probably the biggest handful, stubborn and independent even when very young.

Ruth once put Franklin in the car trunk when he was acting up in a McDonald's drive-through. When she opened it again, he placed his order for a cheeseburger without meat, French fries, and a Coke. He loved never giving his mom the satisfaction of thinking she'd won.

While Graham was traipsing around the world in the name of the Lord, he was firmly grounded in the fact that, just as it is for many parents, his kids were often the very *antithesis of his message, and his wife was home doing the dirty work.*

Today it is a quiet mountain home of wicker and wood, where naps are common, prayer is constant, and two old souls remain deeply in love with each other and their family.

$\mathcal{M}$y family made it in spite of me.[1]

BY THE TIME I FINISHED ALL TWENTY, I MUST HAVE VOMITED FIVE OR SIX TIMES. BUT IT GAVE ME GREAT SATISFACTION NOT TO GIVE IN.[2]

*—**Franklin**, on the time Ruth caught him smoking old cigarette butts when he was little and made him smoke a whole pack*

I regret that I didn't spend more time with my family. I traveled all over the world, I took too many engagements I shouldn't have taken, accepted too many invitations to do various things that, as I look back, have very little meaning in my permanent work.[3]

*W*e decided not to push our son, argue with him, or demand things of him. We just prayed and loved him.[4]

CHILDREN, OBEY YOUR PARENTS BECAUSE YOU BELONG TO
THE LORD, FOR THIS IS THE RIGHT THING TO DO. HONOR THY
FATHER AND MOTHER.

—Ephesians 6:1-2

*W*e understood how difficult it must have been to
have a well-known dad, yet we knew his rebellion was
not against us personally. The girls could marry and
take other names. The boys were stuck with Graham.[5]

*T*he fact that, while we knew that he (Franklin)
smoked, he would never smoke around us revealed this
innate respect. Instead, at home, he would smoke in
his room, blowing the smoke out the window, unaware
the updraft from the valley carried the telltale smell of
cigarette smoke right back to our bedroom window.[6]

IF MOM HAS WHITE HAIR, IT'S BECAUSE OF ME.[7]

—Franklin

*W*hen folks say, "You must be proud of Franklin," we realize that it is not a matter of pride, but of gratitude to God for His faithfulness. With God, nobody's hopeless.[8]

AND THIS IS THE PROMISE: IF YOU HONOR YOUR FATHER AND MOTHER, YOU WILL LIVE A LONG LIFE FULL OF BLESSINGS.

—Ephesians 6:3

*W*hen it comes to preaching, he's a much better preacher than I was at that age. I think God has given him an unusual gift for proclaiming the word of God. And he has a gift of riding horseback and motorcycles and shooting all kinds of guns.[9]

—on his successor, son Franklin

*W*e have another son by the name of Ned who also does great work for God in China, and he has a program going in China that nobody else has. In fact, many missions depend on his contact with the leaders of China. He's made friends with the leadership in China. He lives near Seattle and goes back and forth to China constantly.[10]

DON'T MAKE YOUR CHILDREN ANGRY BY THE WAY YOU TREAT THEM. RATHER BRING THEM UP WITH THE DISCIPLINE AND INSTRUCTION APPROVED BY THE LORD.

—Ephesians 6:4

Thousands of rapt listeners are gathered at Cincinnati's Paul Brown Stadium in June 2002 to hear Billy Graham. Note the big screens at either side. (Photo by Russ Busby)

104

10
Man of the
Real World

How long, Oh Lord, must I call for help, but you do not listen? Violence! I cry, but you do not come to save. Must I forever see this sin and misery all around me? Wherever I look, I see destruction and violence. I am surrounded by people who love to argue and fight. The law has become paralyzed and useless, and there is no justice given in the courts. The wicked outnumber the righteous and justice is perverted with bribes and trickery.

—Habakkuk 1:1-4

As America's Preacher, Graham is often called upon to answer one of the toughest questions that people of God are forced to grapple with. Why does God allow evil in the world?

But in Graham's case, it is almost as if he is having to answer for God. And it is not just fellow Christians who call upon him to ruminate on the issue.

School shootings, celebrity deaths, terrorist attacks, everyday murders and rapes so common they barely make a brief in the newspaper, unless elevated by the bizarre or gruesome nature—the media calls Graham, and a nation listens.

I think we face the same problems that were faced in the first-century man's rebellion against God and God's laws. From the very beginning, when Adam and Eve sinned against God in the Garden of Eden and then their family, Cain and Abel, and Cain killed his brother, Abel—that was the first murder, the first act of violence. Man's been that way ever since.[1]

Jesus was born during the height of the Roman Empire. The Romans built roads from one end of their vast territory to the other—something that had never before happened to such an extent. This enabled the early Christians to spread the news about Jesus across the civilized world in only a few decades—something they never could have done if Jesus had come centuries earlier.[2]

—*on why Jesus wasn't sent to the world sooner, given all the evil*

108

*M*y fondest wish is that the Lord would come back and bring peace to the world, because I am deeply disturbed as I look into the future, about . . . all this new technology that can destroy the human race.[3]

*A*cross Europe at this very hour, there is a stark, naked fear among the people. . . . An arms race unprecedented in the history of the world, is driving us madly toward destruction.[4]

*T*here is another force at work in the world that brings about war and that kind of evil—and that's the devil. In all the discussion we've heard on television and radio, we haven't heard much about the devil.[5]

—*on school violence*

I think we should love them (evildoers), and welcome them, and open our arms to them, and then we don't totally welcome, don't totally accept, them into our fellowship as believers and as Christians until they have repented their sins and changed their way of living.[6]

—*on judging sinners*

'The Bible says that our struggle is not against flesh and blood, but against the powers of this dark world and against the spiritual forces of evil.[7]

*W*e need to take the arms of God into battle every day. It's a daily battle that we face between good and evil.[8]

'There's a power at work. He's called Satan. And there are demons. These demons want to destroy a country like America, or destroy anything that's good in the world. They want to destroy you, they want to destroy me, and they have great power. If it weren't for our faith in God, and the tens of thousands of believers in this country, whether Jews or Catholics or Christians, I think [demons] could overcome this country. But I think it's the religious faith that we have . . . that holds back that terrible power from absolutely bringing anarchy and chaos here in this country.[9]

NOW THE LORD OBSERVED THE EXTENT OF THE PEOPLE'S
WICKEDNESS. HE SAW THAT ALL THEIR THOUGHTS WERE
CONSISTENTLY AND TOTALLY EVIL. SO THE LORD WAS SORRY
HE HAD EVER MADE THEM. IT BROKE HIS HEART.

—Genesis 6:5-6

Evil is real, and most of us have wondered why God
doesn't just reach down and stop it. But He doesn't—
not yet—and the Bible says evil is a mystery we won't
fully understand until we get to heaven.[10]

Our hearts aren't satisfied by materialism. They can't
be. That's why you see someone who has made millions
driven to make more millions. People confuse amassing
money with security. But it is not so. What a pity to
confuse real security with making money.[11]

11
Controversial Man

They encouraged him to continue in the faith, reminding them that they must enter into the kingdom of God through many tribulations.

—Acts 14:22

*G*raham has avoided the roadblocks that have tripped up many other evangelists.

For years, his salary was $69,150, plus $23,050 for housing. In 1992 he got a raise to $101,250, plus $33,750 housing. He was given two homes, one in Florida and one in California, but donated them, to avoid appearances of impropriety.

One wife for life. Yet his words and actions have elicited scorn of both the church and the secular worlds.

Comments about Jews emerged from the Nixon tapes released in 2002. Christian fundamentalists have found him too liberal and don't care for this lifelong Baptist who courts Catholics and admires the Pope.

Of course Graham sins. He is not specific, but hearing a sermon by someone else often prompts him to rededicate his life to Christ. He says he asks God to guard his lips, knowing he is quite capable of misspeaking. When Graham speaks, the words carry plenty of wallop, whether negative or positive.

I believe they are going to nominate the Antichrist.

—when asked in 1948, what he expected the World Council of Churches to do at their upcoming meeting in Copenhagen.

Fundamentalist is a grand and wonderful word. But it got off track and into so many extreme positions.[1]

*I*s AIDS a judgment of God? I could not say for sure, but I think so.

—1993 sermon in Columbus, Ohio

*T*o say God has judged people with AIDS would be very wrong and very cruel. I would like to say that I am very sorry for what I said.[2]

—following the 1993 sermon in Columbus

116

'This stranglehold (of the Jewish media) has got to be broken, or this country's going down the drain.
. . . If you get elected a second time, then we might be able to do something.[3]

—*to President Richard Nixon, 1972*

*A*lthough I have no memory of the occasion (the conversation with Nixon), I deeply regret comments I apparently made in the Oval Office conversation with President Nixon . . . some thirty years ago. They do not reflect my views, and I sincerely apologize for any offense caused by the remarks.[4]

I WAS DISTRAUGHT AND OFFENDED WHEN HE SPENT THE NIGHT IN THE WHITE HOUSE BEFORE BUSH LAUNCHED DESERT STORM. I DON'T THINK THAT'S THE ROLE OF THE CHRISTIAN MINISTER.[5]

—*Alan Neely*, *Princeton Theological Seminary professor*

BILLY CAME TO THE WHITE HOUSE TO GIVE ME THE KIND OF
REASSURANCE THAT WAS IMPORTANT IN DECISIONS AND
CHALLENGES AT HOME AND ABROAD. WHENEVER YOU WERE
WITH BILLY, THERE WAS A SPECIAL FEELING; THERE WAS A
SPECIAL SENSE THAT HE WAS THERE TO GIVE YOU HELP AND
GUIDANCE IN MEETING YOUR PROBLEMS.[6]

—*Gerald Ford*, former U.S. president

THE DIFFERENCE BETWEEN GRAHAM AND OTHERS WAS THAT
HE TOOK CONCRETE STEPS TO PROTECT HIMSELF FROM THOSE
(SEXUAL AND FINANCIAL) TEMPTATIONS. INSTEAD OF SAYING,
"I WON'T FALL AND CAN HANDLE IT," HE SAID, "I MIGHT FALL
AND NEED PROTECTION. THEY (GRAHAM AND HIS ASSOCIATES)
DON'T SAY THAT WE'RE ABOVE SEXUAL TEMPTATION. THEY
TAKE MEASURES TO PUT UP HEDGES AND PROTECT HIM. IT HAS
BEEN A VERY PRACTICAL, PRAGMATIC, REALISTIC APPROACH.[7]

—*William Martin*, Graham biographer

I felt like my own brothers and sisters turned against me.[8]

—*on attacks from fundamentalists*

COUNTERFEIT.

—**Harry Truman**'s assessment of Graham

THE GREATEST PERSON SINCE JESUS.

—**Pat Boone**'s assessment of Graham

[GRAHAM] HAS DONE MORE TO HARM THE CAUSE OF CHRIST THAN ANY OTHER LIVING MAN.

—**Bob Jones III**, fundamentalist leader

AN ICON NOT JUST OF AMERICAN CHRISTIANITY, BUT OF AMERICA ITSELF.

—*William Martin*, *Graham biographer*

I'm a Southern Baptist, and I normally defend my denomination. I'm loyal to it. I believe in them. They have some of the finest people in the world in our denomination. But I have never targeted Muslims. I have never targeted Jews. I believe that we should declare the fact that God loves you. God's willing to forgive you, God can change you, and Christ and His kingdom is open to anybody who repents and by faith receives Him as Lord and Savior.[9]

—*on the Southern Baptist plan to convert Jews and Muslims*

*W*e (Graham and his wife) try to be very careful in what we say and how we live. We try to live in such a way that people will realize that we are Christians and we are living by Christian practice.[10]

12
Old Man

When I first came to you I didn't use lofty words and brilliant ideas to tell you

Now, as you can see, the Lord kept me alive and well as He promised for all these forty-five years since Moses made this promise—even while Israel wandered in the wilderness. Today I am eighty-five years old. I am still as strong now as I was when Moses sent me on that journey, and I can still travel and fight as well as I could then.

—Joshua 14:10-11

In 1993 his doctors at the Mayo Clinic told him he'd be able to preach about five more years. Parkinson's Disease is running its course on the great preacher.

He still had crusades scheduled as of 2002. He is growing frail, however, wishing his body was still up to what his mind can do.

Technically, he has stepped down from the head of the ministry, leaving that to son Franklin.

Graham lies down a few times a day, sometimes just for the energy to take company.

He can no longer write a letter by hand or drive a car. The nation still calls upon him in crisis, as if we need every last day Billy Graham has.

Once helped to the podium, the power in the preaching is still there, making it tough to envision a time when the only Billy Graham we will have will be on tape.

He and Ruth don't like to be apart that much, though Billy still travels when needed.

'The New Testament says nothing of the Apostles who retired and took it easy.[1]

I have Parkinson's Disease, unfortunately. It's a very strange sort of disease because one day you feel fine and the next day you feel way down. You feel like staying in bed all day and then you have trouble walking.[2]

GOD'S NOT FINISHED WITH HIM. HE'S A WARHORSE.[3]

—*Franklin Graham*

I think God has sent it (Parkinson's) at this age to show me that I'm totally dependent on Him.[4]

I've always thought my life would be a short one. I don't think my ministry will be long. I think God allowed me to come for a moment and it will be over, soon.[5]

—*spoken in Pittsburgh, 1952*

*W*ell, you know when you get to be my age, you don't have too many temptations. And I have been offered every kind of thing that you can imagine throughout my life if I would compromise here or compromise the other way. Whether it'd be an office, even of the president of the United States.[6]

*M*y wife was in the hospital . . . for many weeks with spinal meningitis. Been out of the hospital now for about six weeks and I can't keep up with her at all. She goes from morning 'til night. In the middle of the day I have to lie down for a while, to give me strength enough to last the rest of the afternoon. But she's a worker.[7]

*A*fter D. L. Moody was finished, they said the same thing (that he was the last of the big-time evangelists). And after Billy Sunday they said the same thing, and after I'm finished they'll say the same thing. But God will raise up a different one that will do it far better than me.[8]

I don't know why God has allowed me to have this (ministry). I'll have to ask Him when I get to heaven.[9]

I don't think there's been a change as far as the physical stamina in my preaching.[10]

I found that this Parkinson's does slow you down whether you want to slow down or not.[11]

People ask me why our headquarters is in Minneapolis. I was in college there for five years. I went out to see the college while I was up there (summer of 1997) and drove around the grounds. It brought me back a great many memories of the five years I spent there and I learned a great deal.[12]

I had one great failure, and that was intellectual. I should have gone on to school. But I would talk to people about that and they'd say, "Oh, no, go on with what you're doing and let others do that."[13]

It doesn't make me feel any different turning seventy-five than when I turned forty-five. But when I see pictures of my nineteen grandchildren and four great-grandchildren, I know some time has passed. I let days like that slip by and try to forget it. I'm not looking backward, I'm looking to the future.[14]

I've had quite a bit of sickness in my life. But God has helped me through every one of them.[15]

⇒

I stopped two or three times. I said, "I just can't finish it." And my wife agreed with me. She never wanted me to write it in the first place, in the beginning. Now she's glad I did, because she believes God is going to use the book.[16]

—*on writing his memoirs while suffering with Parkinson's Disease*

⇒

I'm looking forward to that moment when I am going to be taken straight into the presence of Christ, in what is called paradise or heaven. And that's going to be a glorious time for me.[17]

⇒

*G*od called me to preach, and I intend to preach as long as I have strength to do so.[18]

⇒

Notes

1 Young Man

1. Graham, Morrow, *They Call Me Mother Graham*. Old Tappan, NJ: Fleming H. Revell, 1977.
2. April 30, 1971 video, World Wide Pictures.
3. Ibid.
4. Ibid.
5. Ibid.
6. Martin, William, *A Prophet with Honor*. New York: William Morrow, 1991.
7. *Billy Graham: The Personal Story of the Man, His Message, and His Mission*. New York: McGraw-Hill, 1956.
8. *American Weekly, Sunday Supplement*, sometime in 1956.
9. Frady, Marshall, *Billy Graham: Parable of American Righteousness*. Boston: Little, Brown, 1979.
10. Martin.
11. Ibid.
12. Ibid.
13. Ibid.
14. Ibid.
15. Ibid.
16. Ibid.
17. *Boston Post*, December 30, 1949.
18. Martin.
19. *Time*, date unknown.
20. Ibid.
21. Ibid.
22. *Legends*, CNN profile, 1986.

23. Pollock, John, *Billy Graham: The Authorized Biography*. New York: McGraw-Hill, 1966.
24. Frady.
25. *Time*, an issue in February 1946.
26. Youth for Christ brochure, September 1947.
27. *Charlotte Observer*, November 23, 1947.
28. *Good Housekeeping*, January 1, 1997.
29. *Saturday Evening Post*, March 1986.
30. *Midwest Today*, January 1997.
31. *Time*, November 15, 1993.
32. Ibid.
33. Source unknown.
34. *Midwest Today*, January 1997.

2 Man of Faith

1. Time online on America Online, July 6, 1999.
2. *Fox News Sunday*, January 1, 2000.
3. *Midwest Today*, January 1997.
4. Time online on America Online, July 6, 1999.
5. *Pittsburgh Press*, September 18, 1952.
6. Graham syndicated column, March 2002.
7. *Eternity*, a 1958 issue.
8. *Good Morning America*, April 30, 1997.
9. Graham syndicated column, March 2002.
10. *Good Morning America*, April 30, 1997.
11. *Midwest Today*, January 1997.
12. Ibid.
13. *American*, January 13, 1950.
14. *Midwest Today*, January 1997.
15. Ibid.
16. *Fox News Sunday*, January 1, 2000.
17. *Good Morning America*, April 30, 1997.

3 Common Man

1. Time online on America Online, July 6, 1999.
2. *Fox News Sunday*, January 1, 2000.
3. Time online on America Online, July 6, 1999.
4. *Fox News Sunday*, January 1, 2000.
5. Ibid.
6. *Midwest Today*, January 1997.
7. *People*, October 14, 1996.
8. *Fox News Sunday*, January 1, 2000.
9. *Sports Illustrated*, August 10, 1992.
10. *Fox News Sunday*, January 1, 2000.

4 Preacher Man

1. Martin, William, *A Prophet with Honor*. New York: William Morrow, 1991.
2. *Time*, November 15, 1993.
3. *Time*, an issue in August 1974.
4. *Charlotte News,* November 10, 1947.
5. *Time*, November 15, 1993.
6. *USA Today*, August 16, 2001.
7. Time online on America Online, July 6, 1999.
8. *Good Morning America*, July 19, 1999.
9. *Calgary Sun*, October 15, 1999.
10. *Midwest Today*, January 1997.
11. *The Record* (Bergen County, New Jersey), August 25, 1991.
12. *Time*, November 15, 1993.
13. *U.S. News & World Report*, December 19, 1988.
14. *Midwest Today*, January 1997.
15. Ibid.
16. *USA Today*, August 16, 2001.
17. *Midwest Today*, January 1997.
18. *The Record* (Bergen County, New Jersey), April 30, 1991.
19. Ibid.

5 Globetrotting Man

1. Martin, William, *A Prophet with Honor.* New York: William Morrow, 1991.
2. *New York Times*, date unknown.
3. *Ladies Home Journal*, date unknown.
4. *Christianity Today*, January 4, 1974.
5. Graham, Billy, *Just as I Am*, Graham biography. New York: HarperCollins, 1997.
6. Source unknown.
7. *Midwest Today*, January 1997.
8. Time online in America Online, July 6, 1999.
9. Martin.
10. *Calgary Sun*, October 15, 1999.
11. *Good Morning America*, July 19, 1999.
12. Ibid.
13. *USA Today*, August 16, 2001.
14. Fox News Sunday, January 1, 2000.
15. *Good Morning America*, April 30, 1997.
16. *The Record* (Bergen County, New Jersey), August 25, 1991.
17. *Calgary Sun*, October 15, 1999.
18. *The Record* August 25, 1991.
19. *Fox News Sunday*, January 1, 2000.
20. Source unknown.
21. *Time*, November 15, 1993.
22. Source unknown.
23. *Time*, November 15, 1993.
24. *Religion Today*, December 20, 1999.
25. *Midwest Today*, January 1997.
26. Ibid.
27. Time online on America Online, July 6, 1999.
28. Ibid.
29. Ibid.
30. *Fox News Sunday*, January 1, 2000.
31. *Good Morning America*, July 19, 1999.

6 Civil Man

1. *Midwest Today*, January 1997.
2. Ibid.
3. *Calgary Sun*, October 15, 1999.
4. Graham syndicated column, March 2002.
5. Ibid.
6. Time online on America Online, July 6, 1999.
7. *Time*, November 15, 1993.
8. Ibid.
9. *Midwest Today*, January 1997.
10. *Good Morning America*, April 30, 1997.
11. *Fox News Sunday*, January 2, 2000.
12. *Midwest Today*, January 1997.
13. *McCall's*, January 1978.

7 Man of Prayer

1. Time online on America Online, July 6, 1999.
2. *Midwest Today*, January 1997.
3. Ibid.
4. Ibid.

8 Man in Love

1. *Good Housekeeping*, September 1, 1997.
2. Time online on America Online, July 6, 1999.
3. *Midwest Today*, January 1997.
4. *Good Housekeeping*, September 1, 1997.
5. Ibid.
6. *People*, February 12, 1996.
7. Ibid.
8. Ibid.
9. Ibid.
10. *Good Housekeeping*, September 1, 1997.
11. Ibid.
12. Ibid.

13. Ibid.
14. Ibid.
15. *Time*, November 15, 1993.
16. *Midwest Today*, January 1997.
17. Ibid.

9 Family Man

1. *People*, October 14, 1996.
2. *Time*, May 13, 1996.
3. *Midwest Today*, January 1997.
4. Time online on America Online, July 6, 1999.
5. *Saturday Evening Post*, April 1996.
6. Ibid.
7. Ibid.
8. Ibid.
9. *Midwest Today*, January 1997.
10. Ibid.

10 Man of the Real World

1. *Midwest Today*, January 1997.
2. Graham syndicated column, March 2002.
3. *Fox News Sunday*, January 1, 2000.
4. *Revival in Our Time*, 1948. Bibliographical information unavailable.
5. Time online on America Online, July 6, 1999.
6. *Fox News Sunday*, January 1, 2000.
7. Time online on America Online, July 6, 1999.
8. Ibid.
9. *Midwest Today*, January 1997.
10. Graham Syndicated column, March 2002.
11. *Midwest Today*, January 1997.

11 Controversial Man

1. *Time*, November 15, 1993.
2. *Cleveland Plain Dealer*, specific 1993 date unknown.
3. Tapes released in March 2002 from the National Archives.
4. Statement released by Graham's Texas public relations firm, March 2002.
5. *Time*, November 15, 1993.
6. Ibid.
7. *The Record* (Bergen County, New Jersey), August 25, 1991.
8. *Time*, November 15, 1993.
9. *Fox News Sunday*, January 1, 2000.
10. *Midwest Today*, January 1997.

12 Old Man

1. *Time*, November 15, 1993.
2. *Midwest Today*, January 1997.
3. *Time*, May 13, 1996.
4. *Midwest Today*, January 1997.
5. *Time*, May 13, 1996.
6. *Fox News Sunday*, January 1, 2000.
7. *Midwest Today*, January 1997.
8. *Time* November 15, 1993.
9. Ibid.
10. *Midwest Today*, January 1997.
11. *Time*, November 15, 1993.
12. *Midwest Today*, January 1997.
13. *Time*, November 15, 1993.
14. Ibid.
15. Time online on America Online, July 6, 1999.
16. *Good Morning America*, April 30, 1997.
17. Ibid.
18. *Midwest Today*, January 1997.

About the Author

*J*ennifer Briggs Kaski has authored several other books, including *Strive to Excel* (featuring Vince Lombardi) and *The Book of Landry* (Tom Landry). She is a long-time sports writer and columnist who has worked for the *Fort Worth Star-Telegram* and the *Wilmington News Journal*. Her work also has appeared in numberous other publications, ranging from *Sports Illustrated* to *Texas Monthly*. Kaski lives near Dallas, Texas.